What parents need to know about MARIJUANA

First printed by Hazelden March, 1983
ISBN: 0-89486-171-9

First published as "FOR PARENTS ONLY:
What You Need to Know About Marijuana
DHHS Publication No. (ADM)81-909
Printed 1980   Revised 1981

Contents

Foreword

Parents today have many questions and concerns about marijuana and its effects on their children's physical and mental health. While we cannot yet answer all of these questions, there are many facts about this drug which we can now share. The following pages contain the latest scientifically accepted information about marijuana. I hope it will be of help to you and the children whose lives you touch.

William Pollin, M.D.
Director
National Institute on Drug Abuse

January 1980

Introduction

Young people today must make decisions about drugs that no previous generation has had to face. And this means that parents too must learn to cope with the reality of a world in which drugs are readily available to their children.

Marijuana in particular is of concern to many parents because of its widespread use and acceptance by many adolescents. Many parents have found that by the time they discover their child uses marijuana, the youngster has been smoking it for years—often to the point where the use of marijuana has become an emotional crutch interfering with schoolwork and social development. The best way to prevent this from happening is to educate yourself about marijuana, learn why and how it is used—and, most important, to leave a line of communication open to your child always.

Unfortunately, this is not always easy. As children reach their teens, the influence of parents is often replaced by the influence of friends. The need to be accepted by others of the same age is very strong; and this peer pressure, this need to belong, has a great influence in marijuana use.

This booklet is written to help you understand what marijuana is, to help you answer your child's questions about it, and to offer some guidelines in effectively handling marijuana experimentation or regular use. It is designed for parents of pre-teens and teens, to give you the information you need to help you discuss marijuana use sensibly with your children.

What You Need to Know About Marijuana Before You Talk With Your Children

There's been a lot of confusion about marijuana. Many years ago, exaggerated stories of the drug's bizarre effects, including tales of violence, amnesia, and sexual frenzy, began to circulate widely. When scientists found no evidence to confirm these rumors, many people began to reject reports of any bad effects of marijuana—and what was considered the "devil's weed" gained a reputation for being a "safe" drug.

This section examines the myths and facts about marijuana. Some of the information may surprise both you and your children. We still do not know everything we would like to know about this controversial drug. But as you will see, our present evidence clearly indicates that it is not a "safe" substance.

Marijuana: What It Is and What It Does

What Exactly Is Marijuana?

Marijuana (also called pot, grass, reefer, or weed) comes from a plant, with the botanical name of *Cannabis sativa,* that grows wild and is cultivated in many parts of the world. Containing over 400 chemicals, this plant has the ability to intoxicate its users, primarily because of the psychoactive or mind-altering ingredient called delta-9-tetrahydrocannabinol, or THC. It is the THC content, found at various concentrations in different parts of the plant, which determines the potency. And the THC content is controlled by plant strain, climate, soil conditions and harvesting.

Typically, the marijuana used in cigarettes (joints) is made from dried particles of the whole plant except the main stem and roots. In 1975, the average confiscated sample of marijuana contained 0.4 percent THC; in 1979, the average THC content was about 4 percent—a tenfold increase. Sinsemilla, a cultivated form of marijuana which is becoming more frequently available in this country, may contain as much as 7 percent THC.

Hashish (hash) is a green, dark brown, or black resin extracted from the *Cannabis sativa* plant and smoked to produce a high. In the past, hashish, which averages about 2 percent THC, contained more THC than marijuana. However, with the increased potency of marijuana on the streets, it now frequently is stronger than hashish.

Hash oil is an extract of the *Cannabis sativa* plant. It may contain up to 30 percent THC, many times the amount found in marijuana. Hash oil is a tarlike substance usually smoked in small amounts on tobacco or marijuana cigarettes or in small pipes.

How Do People Feel When They Smoke Marijuana?

Feelings of euphoria and relaxation are commonly reported as a result of smoking moderate amounts of marijuana. Physically, users experience an increase in heart and pulse rate, a reddening of the eyes, a dryness in the mouth and throat, a mild decrease in body temperature, and, on occasion, a sudden appetite. High doses may result in image distortions and hallucinations.

Many users claim that marijuana enhances their hearing, vision, and skin sensitivity, but these reports have not been confirmed by reseachers. Studies of marijuana's mental effects has shown that the drug temporarily impairs short-term memory, alters the sense of time, and reduces the ability to perform tasks requiring concentration, swift reactions, and coordination.

Do People Ever React Badly to Marijuana?

Yes. The most common adverse reaction to marijuana is a state of anxiety, sometimes accompanied by paranoid thoughts; these can range from general suspicion to a fear of losing control and going crazy. Acute anxiety reactions are usually experienced by novice users, and the symptoms generally disappear in a few hours as the drug's effects wear off. While anxiety reactions can usually be quieted by simple reassurance, some marijuana users may need professional help. Over 11,000 emergency room visits relating to marijuana use were reported in 1979.

Can Marijuana Cause Mental or Psychological Problems?

Marijuana does not directly cause mental problems, but like many other drugs, it appears to bring to the surface emotional problems and can even trigger more severe disorders, particularly schizophrenia. People suffering from depression or other emotional disturbances who use marijuana to treat their symptoms often cause a worsening of the problem. An estimated 5,000 people seek professional treatment every month for problems related to marijuana.

How Can Marijuana Affect Your Child?

In addition to the physical effects described later, a very real danger in marijuana use is its possible interference with growing up. As research shows, the effects of marijuana can interfere with learning by impairing thinking, reading comprehension, and verbal and arithmetic skills.

Scientists also believe that the drug may interfere with the development of adequate social skills and may encourage a kind of psychological escapism. Young people need to learn how to make decisions, to handle success, to cope with failure, and to form their own beliefs and values. By providing an escape from "growing pains," drugs can prevent young people from learning to become mature, independent, and responsible.

How Much Is Heavy Marijuana Use?

For the purpose of this booklet, heavy use is defined as smoking at least once a day. However, many young people when asked to define heavy use say that it means smoking three or more times a day.

What Is Marijuana "Burn Out"?

"Burn out" is a term used by marijuana smokers themselves to describe the effect of prolonged use. Young people who smoke marijuana heavily over long periods of time can become dull, slow moving, and inattentive. These burned-out users, also referred to as "vegged out" or "space cadets," are sometimes so unaware of their surroundings that they do not respond when friends speak to them. Such youngsters, however, do not consider themselves to be burned out. Scientists believe that burn out may be a sign of drug-related mental impairment that may not be completely reversible, or is reversible only after months of abstinence.

Can Marijuana Cause Addiction?

While increasing numbers of people are reporting problems associated with their marijuana use, and many are having problems stopping after heavy or long-term use, there is little evidence that the drug is physically addicting. Animal studies have shown, however, that a tolerance to THC can develop. This means more and more marijuana must be used over time to achieve the high once experienced by using smaller amounts.

Does Marijuana Lead to the Use of Other Drugs?

There is nothing in marijuana itself that causes people to use other drugs. While studies have shown that the use of tobacco and alcohol often precedes marijuana use, the overwhelming majority of marijuana smokers do not go on to use other drugs. But some do; surveys show that the earlier marijuana use begins, the more likely it is that the use will be heavy. Early use also increases the likelihood of subsequent experimentation with other drugs such as hashish, hallucinogens, cocaine, amphetamines, and occasionally barbiturates and heroin.

How Are People Introduced to Marijuana?

Most people are introduced to marijuana by their peers—that is, by people their own age, usually acquaintances or friends. Pushers are rarely involved when a person first smokes marijuana.

How Many People Smoke Marijuana?

Over 50 million Americans have tried marijuana at least once. Approximately 22 million were considered current users at the time of the last national survey in 1979—"current" because they reported smoking marijuana during the month preceding the survey.

A breakdown of teenage marijuana use shows that—

60 percent of high school seniors had tried it, and one out of nine was a daily user;

8 percent of the 12- to 13-year-olds reported that they had smoked marijuana at least once, and half of this group were current users; and

32 percent of the 14- to 15-year-olds had tried it, and 17 percent were still using it.

While children under the age of 12 were not surveyed, many in the 12-to-17 age group report that they first tried marijuana, and even started smoking it regularly, while they were still in grade school—and probably before their parents even suspected they knew about the drug.

What Happens if You Drive After Smoking Marijuana?

Marijuana delays a person's response to sights and sounds—so that it takes a driver longer to react to a dangerous situation.

The ability to perform sequential tasks can also be affected by smoking marijuana. As a result, a marijuana smoker's biggest driving problems occur when faced with unexpected events, such as a car approaching from a side street or a child running out from between parked cars. The greater the demands of a driving situation, the less able the marijuana user will be to cope. The driver who doesn't feel high may still be under the influence of marijuana since its effects may last for several hours after the high has passed.

The combined use of marijuana and alcohol is more hazardous than the the use of either alone. But combined use is becoming widespread; one researcher reported that nearly half of regular marijuana users combine alcohol with marijuana use. Surveys have indicated that from 60 to 80 percent of marijuana users sometimes drive while high.

Marijuana's Effects on the Body

Most of the information on marijuana's effects on the body has been established through studies on both humans and animals, some only by research on animals. Stringent U.S. drug-testing laws require that most research be conducted on men over 18; very few studies have involved women and none have used adolescents.

Marijuana research is relatively new by scientific standards. Many more years and additional studies will be needed before the long-term effects of marijuana use are fully known.

How Long Does Marijuana Stay in the Body After It Is Smoked?

When marijuana is smoked, THC, its active ingredient, is absorbed by many tissues and organs in the body. The body, in its attempt to rid itself of the foreign chemical, chemically transforms the THC into metabolites. Human tests on blood and urine can detect THC metabolites up to a week after marijuana is smoked. Tests involving radioactively labeled THC have traced these metabolites in animals for up to a month.

Can Marijuana Cause Brain Damage?

To date, no definitive neurological study of humans has turned up evidence of marijuana-related permanent brain damage. However, in a recent study of rhesus monkeys, the animals were trained to smoke a marijuana cigarette 5 days a week for 6 months. The researcher reported that persistent changes in the structure of the monkeys' brain cells followed.

This and other studies have led researchers to conclude that the possibility of subtle and lasting changes in brain function from heavy and continuous marijuana use cannot be ruled out.

How Does Marijuana Affect the Heart?

Marijuana use increases the heart rate as much as 50 percent and can bring on chest pain in people already experiencing a poor blood supply to the heart. For this reason, doctors believe that people with heart conditions, or those who are at high risk for heart ailments, should not use marijuana.

How Does Marijuana Affect the Lungs?

Scientists believe that marijuana can be particularly harmful to the lungs because some users inhale the unfiltered smoke deeply and hold it in their lungs as long as possible, thereby keeping the smoke in contact with lung tissue for prolonged periods. Repeated inhalation of smoke, whether marijuana or tobacco, inflames the lungs and affects pulmonary functions. In one study on humans, it was found that smoking five joints a week over time is more irritating to the air passages and impairs the lungs' ability to exhale air than smoking almost six packs of cigarettes a week. Another study on animals using THC levels similar to daily human use found that extensive lung inflammation developed after 3 months to a year of use.

Can Marijuana Cause Cancer?

While marijuana smoke has been found to contain more cancer-causing agents than tobacco smoke, there is no direct evidence so far that marijuana can cause cancer in humans. However, biopsies of human lung tissue chronically exposed to marijuana smoke in a laboratory showed cellular changes called metaplasia that are considered precancerous. In laboratory tests, the tars from marijuana smoke have produced tumors when applied to animal skin.

Does Marijuana Affect the Body's Ability To Fight Infection?

This question remains unresolved. Some reports suggest that white cell formation central to the body's immune response is affected by heavy marijuana smoking. Some laboratory animal studies have found that the immune response is significantly suppressed in mice and rats subjected to high doses of marijuana. Other studies have not confirmed these findings. Because the immune response is so important to good health, long-term studies are essential to determine if marijuana users become more susceptible to disease.

How Does Marijuana Affect the Hormonal and Reproductive Systems?

MEN

A few studies of adult males have found that chronic marijuana users had lower levels of testosterone (the principal male sex hormone) than nonusers, and that abstention from marijuana after heavy use produced a reversal of this condition. Other research has shown that the sperm count in young adult males diminishes as marijuana use increases. Still other studies have shown that some of the sperm of chronic marijuana users are defective and nonfuctional. On the basis of these findings, scientists feel that those with marginal fertility or endocrine functioning should avoid marijuana. In addition, marijuana has been shown to affect the growth hormone from the pituitary. These findings indicate that marijuana may be particularly harmful during adolescence, a period of rapid physical and sexual development.

WOMEN

Information about the reproductive effects of marijuana on women is scarce; marijuana research on women of childbearing age is not permitted because of possible reproductive risks. But one recent study of marijuana use and human female endocrine functioning with 26 women using street marijuana for 6 months or more found they had defective menstrual cycles three times more frequently than a similar group of nonusers. These defective cycles involved either a failure to ovulate or a shortened period of fertility—findings which suggest that regular marijuana use may reduce fertility in women. Many female animal studies have been completed and show that marijuana influences levels of estrogen, the principal female sex hormone, and progesterone, another reproductive hormone, as well as the growth hormone from the pituitary. These studies suggest that heavy use should be avoided by the physically and sexually developing adolescent girl.

Is It OK to Smoke Marijuana if You Are Pregnant?

Definitely not. As stated earlier, research on women is limited because of possible risks to the unborn child. Laboratory animal tests, however, have shown that THC-treated female monkeys were four times more likely than untreated monkeys to abort or have stillborn infants. And males born of the TCH-treated monkeys were lighter than usual in birth weight. Scientists believe that marijuana, which crosses the placental barrier in the pregnant mother's womb, may have a toxic effect on embryos and fetuses. Use of marijuana or any other drug during pregnancy is an unnecessary risk.

What About Breast Feeding?

Animal studies have shown that THC from marijuana can be transmitted to a baby through the mother's milk and that traces of THC have been found in the baby's urine and feces after nursing. Scientists have no doubt that THC is also transmitted in human milk, but because of possible risks to the mother and child, human research has not been done.

Possible Medical Uses of the Chemicals in Marijuana

Research on marijuana has led to findings which indicate some of the plant's chemicals, particularly THC, may have medical value. The following summarizes those areas currently being investigated.

Open-Angle Glaucoma

One of the first potential medical uses of marijuana to be explored was the treatment of open-angle glaucoma. This disease, which often leads to blindness, is caused by pressure within the eye. Marijuana cigarettes, often in combination with standard eye medication, have sometimes reduced this pressure. Synthetically made THC eye drops are also being tested on patients. However, mounting evidence suggests that tolerance (the need to increase amounts to achieve the effects produced by initial doses) develops and that ultimately little or no effect may be realized from the drug.

Use of marijuana does not prevent glaucoma or any other eye disorder, or improve vision.

Nausea

One of the more promising uses of THC is as a means of controlling the overwhelming nausea and vomiting which cancer patients experience during chemotherapy. These side effects sometimes force patients to discontinue necessary treatment. Because the available substances that control these symptoms are not effective for all patients, several research projects are now being sponsored by the federal government and a number of states and independent researchers to further investigate THC's anti-nausea effects.

But marijuana does not prevent cancer. As discussed earlier, marijuana smoke contains more cancer-causing agents than tobacco smoke.

Multiple Sclerosis

Some small studies are being conducted to test whether THC has any effect on reducing spasticity or involuntary muscle contractions in patients with multiple sclerosis. While the results are not conclusive, some patients have shown lowered spasticity after taking the drug. Whether this reduction will make any difference in the patients' ability to function is not yet known.

Epilepsy

A number of human and animal studies have been done to determine if marijuana or any of its ingredients has an effect on epileptic seizures. Some research on THC has shown that it may actually trigger convulsions in epileptics. Scientists hypothesize that this occurs when the drug stimulates high voltage brain waves, and that the likelihood of its happening is determined by the amount of THC in marijuana and the amount inhaled.

Another marijuana ingredient, cannabidiol, has been shown in limited studies to reduce or control seizures. It should be pointed out, however, that cannabidiol is dominant in only one strain of marijuana and that this particular "fiber" strain contains little of the mind-altering THC. This means that the marijuana available for sale on the street contains only trace amounts of cannabidiol. Cannabidiol has been synthesized and is administered orally or by injection to patients involved in studies.

What's a Parent To Do?

Sooner or later, nearly all youngsters find themselves in situations in which they must decide whether or not to take drugs. These decisions are especially hard to make in the midst of conflicting information, peer pressure, curiosity, and the many other influences that are part of adolescence.

If your child has not tried marijuana, consider yourself fortunate, but do not discount the possibility that it could happen sometime in the future. Learn the facts and be prepared to answer questions or deal with the situation if it should occur.

If you think your child has tried marijuana and may even be smoking it regularly, remain calm. Outbursts of anger and emotion are not going to help. They will only interfere with the dialog that is now essential. If you find yourself unable to control your feelings, consider bringing in a third party whose advice and counsel will be respected by both you and your child.

If your child was the one who told you about using marijuana, you should praise him or her for being honest, and be proud that you created the atmosphere that encouraged your child to confide in you. As you discuss marijuana with your son or daughter, try to find out why s/he smokes and how often. The reasons most often cited are, "Because everybody else does" or "It makes me feel good." A closer look may reveal that your child smokes marijuana to avoid rejection by the other kids, to overcome shyness, or to cope with boredom or feelings of failure.

If you suspect your child may be smoking marijuana to get your attention, take a look at your relationship. Perhaps spending more time with your child is called for. Consider planning activities together away from home, school, and business pressures. Try listening and becoming sensitive to your child's feelings and problems, no matter how trivial they seem.

If your child smokes heavily, you might point out the dangers of heavy use and consider seeking help from a doctor or other health professional even if you have to do this without the youngster's consent.

Saying "No"

A recent study with adolescents has shown that teaching them how to say "no" may actually be more important than giving them the reason for saying it. Since peer pressure is so important in drug use, you might consider teaching your child how to handle the time when s/he will be faced with making a decision about marijuana or other drugs.

Guilt Doesn't Help

Don't feel guilty or ashamed about your child's marijuana use. Even children of loving parents who have set a good example and taught moderation can become caught up in drug use. Peer group pressure is often strong enough to override the best parental influences.

As you try to cope with the "hows" and "whys" of marijuana, it is important to remember that children are not the only ones who have peers. Your own friends, your neighbors, and the parents of your child's friends are facing the same problems and asking the same questions.

Talk About Drugs With Other Parents

If you know your child's friends are smoking marijuana and you would like to do something to stop it, start by inviting their parents to your home one evening. Tell them of your concerns and share all the information you have. Some will probably report similar experiences and may be relieved to find someone who shares their troubles and will work with them to look for solutions.

Some parents may become defensive and insist that marijuana use is not a problem in their families. This is a natural reaction for people who are frightened and confused. For many, a stigma is still attached to marijuana use. They believe that drugs are used only by "bad" children of "unfit" parents.

At any parent meeting try to avoid accusations and blame—"your child does this," "well, *your* child does that." Remember that the purpose of a parent group is cooperation and sharing.

Establish Uniform Rules for the Peer Group

An approach some parents have tried is establishing uniform rules to make access to drugs harder. If you and the parents of your child's friends can agree on appropriate curfews, limits on spending money and use of the family car, and other guidelines, the young people in your community will not be able to justify or excuse their behavior by saying, "But all the other kids are allowed to!" This will also help develop a sense of an extended family in the community where the parents cooperate and the young people are treated alike.

Parent groups that have tried this approach report that:

Their children seem more active and attentive, and their grades improve.

Their youngsters are now voluntarily following rules that they used to think were unreasonable.

The parent-child relationship is better than ever.

Younger children are not falling into the same drug-oriented culture which influenced their older brothers and sisters.

Develop Alternatives to Drug Use

There are any number of healthy activities which can show your child how to have a good time without being high on a drug. Whenever possible, do them together. Here are some examples:

Running	Gardening
Music	Furniture-Making
Painting	
Theater	Hockey
Boating	Skating
Soccer	Dancing
Skiing	Basketball
Macrame	Tennis
Gymnastics	Biking
Camping	Cooking

Remember, what is most important is not the activity but that you are taking a personal interest and that your child is developing a focus on things other than drugs.

Marijuana Jargon

Parents today are trying to cope not only with marijuana but also with the drug's vocabulary. While drug terms are continually changing and are often different in various parts of the country, this list may help you decipher the most popular marijuana jargon.

Acapulco Gold—a potent strain of marijuana with gold or yellow highlights.

Bong—a cylindrical water pipe used to smoke marijuana.

Burn out—a slang term for a state of apathy and deadened perceptions which can result from habitual use of marijuana.

Buzz—slang term for a high or a drug-induced euphoria.

Colombian—a potent strain of marijuana.

Decriminalization—process of reducing penalties for personal use of marijuana from prison sentences to civil fines.

Dime—a quantity of drugs which sells on the streets for $10.

Dope—slang term for marijuana and other drugs.

Duster—cigarette made of tobacco, mint leaves, marijuana, or parsley sprinkled with phencyclidine (PCP), also know as Angel Dust.

Ganja—a potent form of *Cannabis* obtained from the flowering tops and leaves of the plant. It may also be used to refer to marijuana in general.

Grass—slang term for marijuana.

Hashish—a form of *Cannabis* made either from the *Cannabis sativa* plant or its resin.

Hash oil—a form of *Cannabis* which is extracted or distilled from the *Cannabis sativa* plant.

Head shops—stores which specialize in the sale of drug paraphernalia and drug-related items.

High—a widely used slang term for euphoria and intoxication.

Hit—a single drag or inhalation of marijuana smoke.

Joint—a hand-rolled marijuana cigarette.

Killer weed—slang term for PCP-treated parsley or marijuana.

Loaded—slang term for state of being high or intoxicated.

Nickel—a quantity of marijuana which sells on the street for $5.

Ounce—a standard unit of measurement for marijuana.

Paraphernalia—drug equipment or gadgets usually sold in head shops.

Pot—slang term for marijuana.

Reefer—slang term for marijuana.

Roach—the small end of a marijuana joint which remains after most of the cigarette is smoked.

Roach clip—a device used to hold the roach or the tail end of a marijuana joint.

Rolling papers—cigarette papers used to make a marijuana joint.

Scales—paraphernalia used to weigh drug quantities for selling purposes.

Smoking stones—paraphernalia used to hold marijuana joints while smoking.

Space cadet—slang term for a habitual marijuana user whose senses have become dulled.

Spaced out—slang term for a drug-induced state of being lost or out of touch with surroundings.

Stash—any container or place used to store marijuana or other drugs.

Stoned—slang term for being high or intoxicated from marijuana.

Supergrass—slang term for marijuana treated with phencyclidine (PCP or Angel Dust).

Toke—slang term for an inhalation of marijuana or hashish smoke.

Water pipe—paraphernalia used to smoke marijuana or hashish which filters the smoke through water.

Weed—slang term for marijuana.

Common Drugs of Abuse

CATEGORY	Drugs	Sample trade or other names	Medical uses	Dependence Physical	Psychological
CANNABIS	Marijuana	Pot, grass, reefer, sinsemilla			
	Tetrahydrocannabinol	THC	Under investigation	Unknown	Moderate
	Hashish	Hash			
	Hash oil	Hash oil	None		
DEPRESSANTS	Alcohol	Liquor, beer, wine	None	High	High
	Barbiturates	Secobarbital, Amobarbital, Butisol, Tuinal	Anesthetic, anti-convulsant, sedative, hypnotic	High-moderate	High-moderate
	Methaqualone	Quaalude, Sopor, Parest	Sedative, hypnotic	High	High
	Tranquilizers	Valium, Librium, Equanil, Miltown	Anti-anxiety, anti-convulsant, sedative	Moderate to low	Moderate
STIMULANTS	Cocaine	Coke, flake, snow	Local anesthetic		
	Amphetamines	Biphetamine, Dexedrine	Hyperactivity, narcolepsy	Possible	High
	Nicotine	Tobacco, cigars cigatettes		High	Low
	Caffeine	Coffee, tea, cola drinks, No-Doz	None	Low	Low
HALLUCINOGENS	LSD	Acid			Degree unknown
	Mescaline and peyote	Button, Cactus	None	None	
	Phencyclidine	PCP, angel dust	Veterinary anesthetic	Unknown	High
	Psilocybin-psilocin	Mushrooms	None	None	Degree unknown
INHALANTS	Nitrous oxide	Whippets, laughing gas	Anesthetic		
	Butyl nitrite	Locker room, rush	None		
	Amyl nitrate	Poppers, snapper	Heart stimulant	Possible	Moderate
	Chlorohydrocarbons	Aerosol paint, cleaning fluid	None		
	Hydrocarbons	Aerosol propellants gasoline, glue paint thinner	None		
NARCOTICS	Opium	Paregoric	Antidiarrheal, pain relief	High	High
	Morphine	Morphine, Pectoral Syrup			
	Codeine	Codeine, Empirin Compound with Codeine, Robitussin A-C	Pain relief, cough medicine	Moderate	Moderate
	Heroin	Horse, smack	Under investigation	High	High
	Methadone	Dolophine Methadose	Heroin substitute, pain relief	High	High

Effects in hours	Possible effects	Effects of overdose	Withdrawal symptoms
2-4	Euphoria, relaxed inhibitions, increase in heart and pulse rate, reddening of the eyes, increased appetite, disoriented behavior	Anxiety, paranoia, loss of concentration, slower movements, time distortion	Insomnia, hyperactivity, and decreased appetite occasionally reported
1-12 1-16 4-8	Slurred speech, disorientation, drunken behavior	Shallow respiration, cold and clammy skin, dilated pupils, weak and rapid pulse, coma, possible death	Anxiety, insomnia, tremors, delirium, convulsions, possible death
½-2 2-4	Increased alertness, excitation; euphoria, increase in pulse rate and blood pressure, insomnia, loss of appetite	Agitation, increase in body temperature, hallucinations, convulsions, possible death, tremors Agitation, increase in pulse rate and blood pressure, loss of appetite, insomnia	Apathy, long periods of sleep, irritability, depression
8-12 Variable 6	Illusions and hallucinations, poor perception of time and distance	Drug effects becoming longer and more intense, psychosis	Withdrawal symptoms not reported
Up to ½ hr.	Excitement, euphoria, giddiness, loss of inhibitions, aggressiveness, delusions, depression, drowsiness, headache, nausea	Loss of memory, confusion, unsteady gait, erratic heart beat and pulse, possible death	Insomnia, decreased appetite, depression irritability, headache
3-6 12-24	Euphoria, drowsiness, respiratory depression, constricted pupils, nausea	Slow and shallow breathing, clammy skin, convulsions, coma, possible death	Watery eyes, runny nose, yawning, loss of appetite, irritability, tremors, panic, chills and sweating, cramps, nausea